See Them Grow

DRAGONFLY

by Anastasiya Vasilyeva

Consultant: Dr. Robin Elizabeth Thomson
Curator, Insect Collection
Department of Entomology, University of Minnesota
St. Paul, Minnesota

BEARPORT
PUBLISHING

New York, New York

Credits

Cover, © Skip Moody/Dembinsky Photo Associates/Alamy and © Tatiana Volgutova/Shutterstock; Title Page, © Tom Biegalski/Shutterstock; TOC, © Alex Uralsky/Shutterstock; 3TR, © Tom Biegalski/Shutterstock; 4, © Debra Rade/iStock; 5, © Tom Biegalski/Shutterstock; 6–7, © Henryhartley/CC BY 3.0/Wikipedia; 8, © Brian Lasenby/Shutterstock; 9, © All Canada Photos/Alamy; 10–11, © BRUCE COLEMAN INC./PHOTOSHOT/Alamy; 12–13, © Vitalii Hulai/Shutterstock; 14, © WildPictures/Alamy; 15, © Gary Meszaros/Science Source; 16, © blickwinkel/Alamy and © waldru/Shutterstock; 17T, © Mike Truchon/Shutterstock; 17B, © JIANG HONGYAN/Shutterstock; 18, © blickwinkel/Alamy; 19, © David Lester/Alamy; 20–21, © Paul Reeves Photography/Shutterstock and © llaszlo/Shutterstock; 22, © Marvin Dembinsky Photo Associates/Alamy; 23 (T to B), © Isselee/Dreamstime, © Worraket/Shutterstock, © Mathisa/Shutterstock, © Henryhartley/CC BY 3.0/Wikipedia, © TommyIX/iStock, and © JapanNature/iStock; 24, © Melinda Fawver/Shutterstock.

Publisher: Kenn Goin
Editor: Jessica Rudolph
Creative Director: Spencer Brinker
Design: Debrah Kaiser
Photo Researcher: Thomas Persano

Library of Congress Cataloging-in-Publication Data

Names: Vasilyeva, Anastasiya, author.
Title: Dragonfly / by Anastasiya Vasilyeva.
Description: New York, New York : Bearport Publishing, 2017. | Series: See them grow | Includes bibliographical references and index. | Audience: Ages 5 to 8.
Identifiers: LCCN 2016038817 (print) | LCCN 2016047755 (ebook) | ISBN 9781684020393 (library) | ISBN 9781684020911 (ebook)
Subjects: LCSH: Dragonflies—Life cycles—Juvenile literature.
Classification: LCC QL520 .V37 2017 (print) | LCC QL520 (ebook) | DDC 595.7/33—dc23
LC record available at https://lccn.loc.gov/2016038817

For more information, write to Bearport Publishing Company, Inc., 45 West 21st Street, Suite 3B, New York, New York 10010. Printed in the United States of America.

10 9 8 7 6 5 4 3 2 1

Contents

Dragonfly

An **insect** zooms over a pond.

It's a dragonfly!

The creature has big eyes, a long body, and large wings.

How did it get that way?

Dragonflies eat other insects, like mosquitoes. They often catch their food while they're flying!

In the fall, a male dragonfly flies over a pond.

He looks for a female.

When he finds one, the two **mate**.

Some dragonflies spend the fall traveling to warmer places. These dragonflies mate in the winter months.

male

female

After mating, the female finds a water plant, such as a lily pad.

She makes a cut in the plant.

Then she lays her eggs inside.

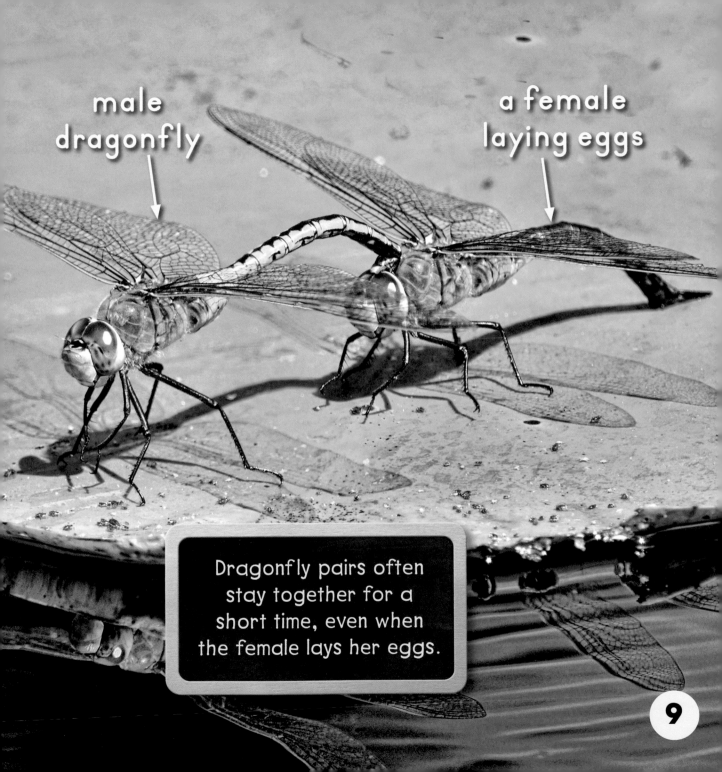

male
dragonfly

a female
laying eggs

Dragonfly pairs often
stay together for a
short time, even when
the female lays her eggs.

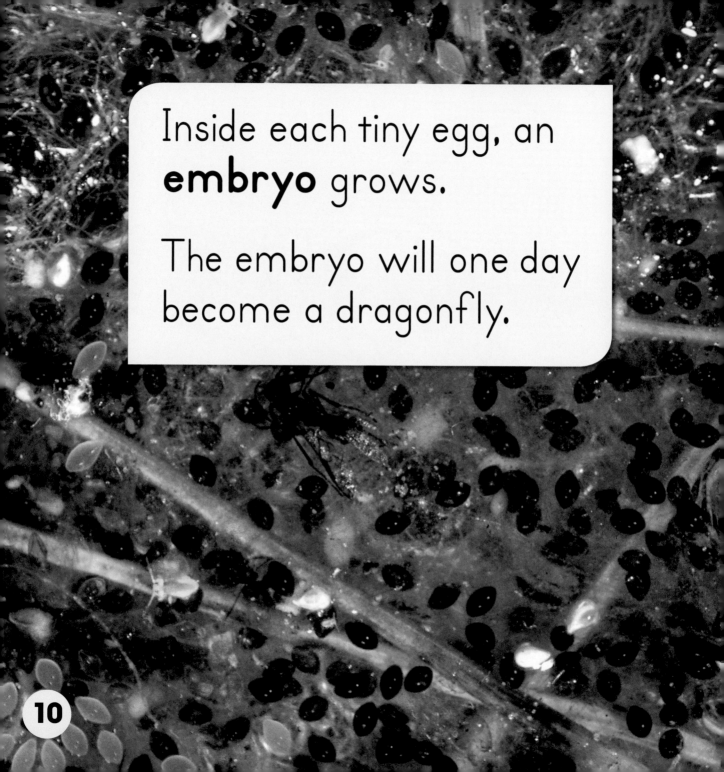

Inside each tiny egg, an **embryo** grows.

The embryo will one day become a dragonfly.

10

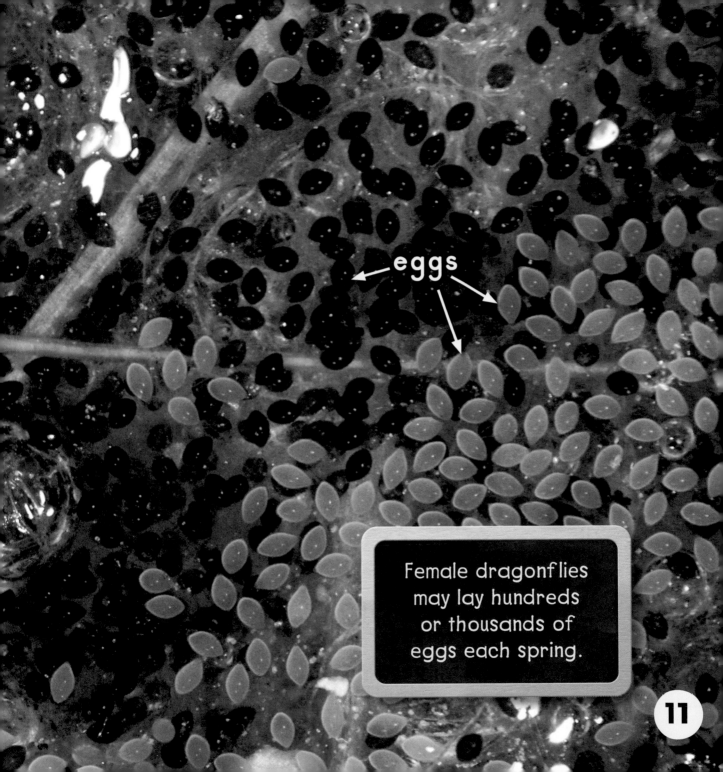

eggs

Female dragonflies may lay hundreds or thousands of eggs each spring.

11

Nymphs hatch from the eggs a few days after they were laid.

Then they break through the plant surrounding the eggs to reach the water.

Nymphs swim by squirting water out from the ends of their bodies!

Nymphs have greenish-brown **exoskeletons.**

13

A nymph needs to eat a lot to grow.

It feeds on other insects in the water.

a baby
mosquito

a nymph
eating

Sometimes it feeds on tiny fish and tadpoles, too.

Just like fish, nymphs breathe through body parts called gills.

fish

15

For about a year, the nymph grows and grows.

When it gets too big for its skin, the nymph sheds it.

This is called **molting**.

The nymph molts 6 to 15 times.

old skin

A nymph's color helps it blend in with rocks and water plants. This way, it can hide from animals that try to eat it, such as frogs and birds.

17

After a year, the nymph crawls out of the water for a final molt.

Its exoskeleton breaks open.

A dragonfly with wings wriggles out!

The dragonfly flaps its wings back and forth. This helps the wings get strong for the insect's first flight.

old skin

dragonfly

Soon, its wings are strong enough.

The young dragonfly takes off!

For a few weeks, the insect eats and gets stronger.

Then, it can mate and have its own young.

Green darners are one of the biggest kinds of dragonflies. Their wings can stretch 4.5 inches (11.4 cm) from end to end.

Dragonfly Facts

- Dragonflies are very fast. They can fly up to 35 miles (56 km) per hour.

- There are thousands of different kinds of dragonflies.

- As nymphs, green darners live for about a year. As dragonflies, they live up to a month.

- Dragonflies can hover in the air like a helicopter!

Glossary

 **embryo** (EM-bree-oh) an animal in the first stage of development

 **exoskeletons** (*eks*-oh-SKEL-uh-tuhnz) hard outer coverings that protect the bodies of some animals such as insects

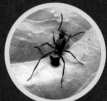 **insect** (IN-sekt) a small animal that has six legs, three main body parts, two antennae, and an exoskeleton

 **mate** (MAYT) to come together to have young

 **molting** (MOHLT-ing) shedding an old skin called an exoskeleton so a new one can form

 **nymphs** (NIHMFS) young dragonflies that live in water

Index

Read More

Glaser, Linda. *Dazzling Dragonflies: A Life Cycle Story.* Minneapolis, MN: Lerner (2008).

Lawrence, Ellen. *A Dragonfly's Life (Animal Diaries: Life Cycles).* New York: Bearport (2013).

Learn More Online

To learn more about dragonflies, visit
www.bearportpublishing.com/SeeThemGrow

About the Author

Anastasiya Vasilyeva lives in New York City.
She loves to spot dragonflies at the park on sunny days.